I0188672

Beaufort, North Carolina aerial view. *Courtesy of Diane Hardy and Tom Randy.*

CARTERET COUNTY

NORTH CAROLINA

HISTORY & FOLKLORE

MARY & GRAYDEN PAUL

The
History
PRESS

Published by The History Press
Charleston, SC 29403
www.historypress.net

First published 2008

ISBN 9781540229267

Library of Congress Cataloging-in-Publication Data
Paul, Mary C.
Carteret County, North Carolina : history & folklore / Mary and Grayden Paul ;
sponsored by Beaufort Historical Association.
p. cm.
ISBN 9781540229267
1. Carteret County (N.C.)--History--Anecdotes. 2. Beaufort (N.C.)--History--Anecdotes.
3. Carteret County (N.C.)--Biography--Anecdotes. 4. Beaufort (N.C.)--Biography-
-Anecdotes. 5. Folklore--North Carolina--Carteret County. 6. Folklore--North
Carolina--Beaufort. 7. Carteret County (N.C.)--Songs and music. 8. Beaufort
(N.C.)--Songs and music. 9. Beaufort (N.C.)--Tours. I. Paul, Grayden. II. Beaufort
Historical Association. III. Title.
F262.C23P38 2008
975.6'197--dc22
2008022616

CONTENTS

FOREWORD

The authors of *Carteret County, North Carolina: History & Folklore*, Grayden and Mary Clark Paul, were an inseparable team for almost seventy-five years. Grayden died at the age of ninety-five in 1994 and two years later Mary died at the age of ninety-seven. Their story is as interesting as the book they wrote.

Grayden was born in the small "down-east" community of Davis, North Carolina. His family subsequently moved to Beaufort, where his father opened a machine shop and the first motion picture theater in Carteret County. Mary Clark Wilhelm was born in Bradenton, Florida, and her family later moved to St. Petersburg, Florida, where her father established a flourishing mortuary business.

Grayden and "M.C." met when she came to Beaufort to visit her sister, who was the wife of the new pastor of the First Baptist Church. Their meeting was almost love at first sight, as they were married shortly thereafter. With the exception of a few excursions to Florida, they lived the rest of their lives in Beaufort. Here they raised their family and made their lasting mark on the community.

Grayden was a businessman and a civic leader. He had his own machine shop and marine railways business. He was mayor of Beaufort and was head of civil defense for the county during World War II. He was one of the founders of the Beaufort Historical Association, where he initiated and was the narrator of the famous double-decker bus tours of Beaufort. Grayden was also responsible for and coordinated the 250th celebration of the founding of Beaufort. He opened the first Maritime Museum in Beaufort as a private venture, and he was a deacon as well as a Sunday school teacher at the First Baptist Church, just to name a few of his many activities. M.C. was always at his side, helping with her husband's various endeavors. Grayden's true love, however, was recounting the folklore tales and songs that had been handed down by his parents and grandparents. Grayden and M.C. performed many times at various social and civic events, with Grayden telling the tales and singing the songs, while M.C. played accompaniment on the piano. (M.C. was an accomplished pianist and organist.) Many people asked why the pair did not put down their marvelous tales and songs in writing, and they finally decided to do just that. The result is this charming little book, which I hope you will thoroughly enjoy reading.

Grayden Paul Jr.

The eldest son of Grayden and M.C. Paul, Grayden is a retired aerospace executive who now resides in Beaufort, where he was born and raised.

PREFACE

Courtesy of the Beaufort Historical Association.

The purpose of this book is not to recall facts or dates of history (though some names and dates are correct); rather, it is to preserve for future generations certain folklore tales and songs that were handed down to me by my parents and grandparents. These stories are actual happenings in the lives of seafaring, God-fearing people who lived, loved and died on the sandy, windswept shores of Carteret County for 250 years or more.

This is a reproduction of a sketch that my wife and I have performed many times for civic events in Carteret County. I sang the songs while my wife played my accompaniment on the piano. So far as I know, the tunes of these songs were never written out in notes, but were handed down from generation to generation.

We have been requested by so many people to have it put in book form that we are now attempting to do so, and are dedicating this book to our children, Grayden Jr., Harry Allan and Mary Frazier, hoping that they will keep it alive for another generation.

Mr. G.M. Paul
Sunshine Court
Beaufort, North Carolina
March 8, 1972

HISTORICAL FACTS
ABOUT CARTERET
COUNTY

There are records in the Register of Deeds Office in New Bern, North Carolina, attesting to the fact that in 1708, a grant of 780 acres of land was given to Furnival Green. When a grant of land was made, it carried certain stipulations. Some of the land was to be cleared, and certain buildings were to be erected within a given time, or the land would go back to the Crown. Green apparently was unable to fulfill the conditions of the land grant, so in 1713, he obtained permission to sign over his patent to Robert Turner for seven pounds, fifteen shillings.

Turner was a promoter, and immediately had two hundred acres of his land surveyed by Richard Graves, the deputy surveyor of the colony. These two hundred acres Turner name Beaufort, for the Duke of Beaufort, of England. Turner went about naming the streets of his town. He started on the west side, and named this street Moore for Colonel Moore. The next street he named Orange for the Duke of Orange, and the ruling family of England. Turner Street he named for himself, and here he planned the hub of activity for his town. A natural spring at the south end of the street was used to make a watering place for horses. A stagecoach stop, a place for tethering horses, customs house, courthouse, general store, slave block and a boat landing were planned for this street. Large ships were to anchor in the sound, and small boats and barges were used to bring wares ashore at the south end of Turner Street. Craven Street was named for the earl of Craven of England; Queen Street was named for Queen Ann of England; and Pollock Street for Governor Pollock of North Carolina (one of the state's wealthiest men). This is as far east as Turner had planned. Ann Street, running east and west, Turner named for the ruler of England. It is not documented fact, but tradition says Queen Anne was so pleased that a street in the New World was named for her that she set aside a perpetuation sum of money to have elm trees planted on this street. Front Street was not planned. It was only a footpath along the shore, and years later gained its name by usage.

Turner also became discouraged with his plans and the isolation of this location, so a few years later, in 1720, he sold his land to Richard Rustull. Soon after, Rustull sold to Nathaniel Taylor in 1725. Part of Turner's dream came true in 1722, when Beaufort became an incorporated town, and the assembly established Beaufort as a "Port of Entry."

Beaufort Township exchanged hands six times in a period of thirty-six years: Robert Turner sold to Richard Rustull in 1720; Richard Rustull sold to Nathaniel Taylor in 1725; Nathaniel Taylor sold to Thomas Martin in 1733; Thomas Martin sold to John Pinder in 1739; and John Pinder sold to James Winright in 1744.

Many famous and important people have lived in Carteret County. Once of the earliest was Chief Justice Christopher Gale, who lived here from 1722 to 1724. Later he became a member of the legislature. He may have been influential in establishing Beaufort as a "Port of Call." Liggett, ancestor of Liggett-Myers fame, owned

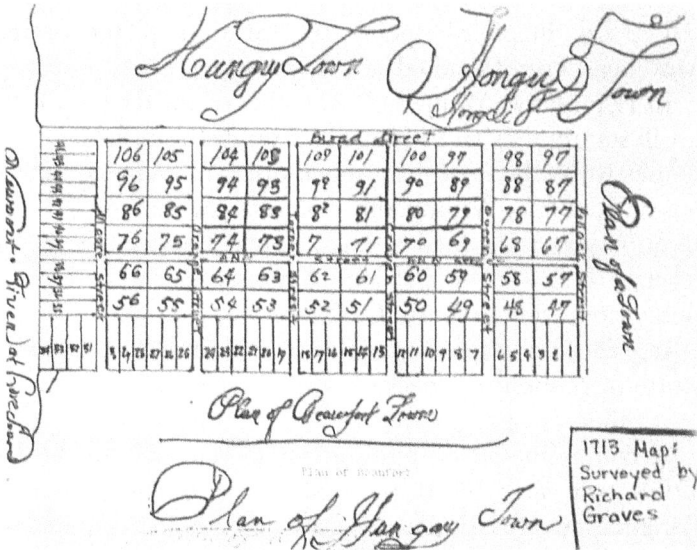

Sketched by surveyor Richard Graves in 1713, this is the original plan for the town of Beaufort. Many of the original street names remain unchanged. *Courtesy of the Beaufort Historical Association.*

the Hammock House at one time. The Bordens, Quakers and ancestors of Borden Milk Company, also lived in the Hammock House. The Bordens were outstanding boat builders of that day.

In the late 1700s, Jacob Shepherd built and lived in the house on Front Street now owned by Mrs. Roland Bell. Beaufort was then a "Port of Call." A Captain Charles Biddle, on a visit to Beaufort on a run from Philadelphia to the Bahamas, met and fell in love with Hannah Shepherd, the daughter of Jacob Shepherd. Charles Biddle and Hannah Shepherd were married. He was of the Biddle family who established the great banding firm of Philadelphia. Hannah Shepherd was a member of the Shepherd family who later settled on Shepherd's point, the location of the present Morehead Port Terminal.

In 1744, James Wainwright, member of the legislature, left a will stating that all the rents and profits from his land and houses would be used for a sober, discreet, qualified man to teach "Reading, Writing and Common Arithmetic." A sum of $250 was to be used to build a school and house for the teacher. This was the first sum of money ever to be given to public education in North Carolina.

In 1780, the general assembly levied a tax on every $500 worth of property—a peck of corn, three pounds of salt port or a gallon of salt.

A common way of punishment for convicts in the late 1700s and early 1800s, particularly negro slaves from the Bahamas, was to lash the felons a stated number of times and then banish them to the West Indies. Sometimes felons were branded on their thumbs with a letter commensurate with the crime they had committed.

Smallpox was brought into Carteret County from the West Indies. It was raging in 1825 and strict laws regarding the disease were made. There was terrible ignorance of the nature of the malady. The land of Front Street extended about a mile from the post office, and there was a pond called Smallpox Pond. Here huts and tents were set up to house the smallpox victims in isolation. Few survived.

Commander James Cooke, of the ram ironclad *Albemarle*, was born in Beaufort on Front Street at the site of the Julius Duncan Sr. house, and lived in the Hammock House when he was about nineteen years old.

Captain Otway Burns, the blockade runner, after the War of 1812 built and lived in the house on North River Road that Mr. and Mrs. Robert King now own. Burns had a canal dug from North River to his property, and brought to his house produce by barge from his ship anchored in the river.

Major General Ambrose Burnside, commander of the Federal troops in North Carolina during the Civil War, lived on Queen Street in the house now owned by Reverend Stanley Potter.

The father of Edwin M. Stanton, secretary of war under Lincoln, was born at Core Creek. The house is still standing and occupied.

Christian Tupper wrote the novel *Adventuring* about Beaufort, and used local people as his characters.

At this crucial point in the War Between the States, the Federal government made a deal with prisoners who were serving life terms, guaranteeing them that if they would fight in the Union army until the war was over, they would be given their freedom. Many prisoners agreed to this.

During the Civil War, when the Federal army occupied Beaufort, a company of volunteers calling themselves Zouaves was sent from the North to Beaufort. They adopted the colorful costumes of the Zouave mercenaries of Algeria. They wore red fezzes, black boots and red pantaloons. They came to Beaufort for the purpose of training men in an unusual form of warfare.

These Zouaves were a fierce group of warriors who fought with knives in an unusual manner. They used a knife with a blade about ten inches long. The handle was four inches long, with a hole in the end through which was tied an elastic band ten or twelve feet long. One end of this band was tied to the wrist of the soldier so that the knife could be thrown, inflicting a mortal wound, and the weapon could be retrieved by use of the rubber band. This was where the skill and danger of the training came, because in retrieving the knife, the trainee had to be able to receive the knife without injuring himself.

A training camp for this purpose was set up on the Courthouse Square, around a pond that was there at the time. Dummies were set up on one side of the pond and the trainees were lined up on the other side, about twelve feet away. They practiced throwing their knives at the dummies, and in the process of retrieving the knives they often cut themselves on their arms and hands.

The source of information for this story comes from Charlie Glover, whose grandmother stood and watched the trainees practice on many occasions. She said the water in the pond often turned red with blood from the wounds of the men, but when their training was over, they were able to retrieve the knives without a scratch. We have no knowledge that these Zouave trainees were ever called into this form of battle.

THE FIRST
INHABITANTS OF
CARTERET COUNTY

So far as we know, the American Indians were the first human beings to roam the coast and woodlands of Carteret County. From whence they came or how long they had been here when the white man arrived is not known; but we do know that Indian artifacts have been found in the same excavations with remains of the wooly mammoth and mastodons, which roamed the continent before the birth of Christ.

There were three tribes living here when Ralph Lane and his English explorers first landed at Cape Lookout in 1585. The Hatteras tribe lived on the Outer Banks and Harkers Island. Cape Hatteras was named for them. The Corees lived on the mainland bordering Core Sound, which gets its name from them. The Neuse tribe lived around the mouth of the Neuse River, which was named for them.

The Indians must have been very fond of oysters, judging by the tremendous oyster shell mound that old-timers can recall jutting out from the east end of Harkers Island, almost halfway across Core Sound. Even today, from an airplane, the outline of what seems to be a footpath can be seen all the way to Core Banks, so no doubt the Indians were to first to build a roadway to the Outer Banks.

When the white man found that these shells could be used for making lime and paving roads, large sailing vessels from Boston, New York and Virginia started coming and hauling them away until the roadway was finally destroyed; centuries later, people were still finding Indian arrowheads at Shell Point.

The Indians had very few musical instruments except war drums and tom-toms, but the white man wrote many songs about the Indians. One such song is "Little Mohee."

It was not until the dawn of the eighteenth century that white men first began to settle along the North Carolina coast. In 1709, some French Huguenots settled in a spot that was suitable for their trade as fishermen. They had easy access to the ocean through Old Topsail Inlet (later to be named Beaufort Inlet). They called their settlement Fish Town. It had such great promise that they soon changed the name to Paradise.

The Indians were friendly at first, but after some mistreatment by the white men, they joined with their more warlike neighbors, the Tuscaroras, who lived around New Bern, and started an Indian war in 1711. This "Tuscaroran massacre," as it was called, killed off most of the early settlers along the coast. Had it not been for the arrival of Colonel Maurice Moore and his colonial troops from Charles Town, South Carolina, the settlers would have all been killed. The survivors were so grateful for Moore's help that they named one of the streets for him. Things were so bad for the next few years that they also changed the name of their settlement from Paradise to Hungry Town.

While all this was happening on the mainland, a group of hardy souls was beginning to settle along a strip of the outer banks that we know today as Shackleford Banks, which runs from Cape Lookout to Beaufort Inlet, a distance of eight miles; this is the only strip of beach on the Atlantic Coast that runs east to west. These people made their living from the sea—therefore, they had to live close to the sea. They were whalers and boat builders, and a few "had-been" pirates; for it was in 1718 when Blackbeard the pirate left one of his three boats with seventeen men at Cape Lookout to be repaired while he went on to Edenton to keep his annual infamous rendezvous with Governor Eden. He was to pick these men up on the way back south, but when they heard that he had been killed, they decided to give up the life of piracy and settle down to an honest way of life.

In 1724, Samuel Chadwick came down from New England and started a whale fishery that stayed in continuous operation until 1898. He was the forefather of most of the Chadwicks in Carteret County today.

Other early comers included John Royal, who helped build the present Cape Lookout Lighthouse and became its first keeper. He was the great-great-grandfather of our beloved Dr. Ben Royal, who was born on Shackleford Banks. Dr. Royal is now deceased.

There were several communities during the height of the whaling business, including Wade's Shore, Windsor's Lump, Guthrie's Hammock and the Mullet Pond. But when the lighthouse was completed and painted with its famous white and black diamond shapes, they all came together in one large community, and called it Diamond City. However, it did not last long. Whaling soon lost out to an easier way of life, and the residents began to move over to the mainland. By 1900, only a few families lived on the Banks, and Diamond City became the Lost City of Shackleford Banks.

LITTLE MOHEE

As I sat amusing myself in the shade
Oh, who should come near me but a fair Indian maid.
She sat down beside me, took hold of my hand;
She said, "You're a stranger and not of our band.

But if you will follow, you are welcome to go
And share with me always my pleasures and woe.
Together we'll ramble, together we'll roam;
Till we come to a little Wigwam that we can call Home."

But my dearest fair maiden, this never can be;
For I have a true-love in my native Coun-try
Forsake her I'll never; a true lover I'll be,
For her heart's just as true as the little Mohee.
But when I was safe landed on my own native shore,
With friends and companions gathered round me once more,
I looked all around me but none could I see,
That I could compare with my little Mohee.

So if you will follow you are welcome to go
And share with me always my pleasures and woe.
Together we'll ramble, together we'll roam;
Till we come to a little Wigwam that we can call Home.

THE LAST WHALE
KILLED ALONG THESE
SHORES

It was April 3, 1898. The sun came up over the Atlantic Ocean with a burst of glory. The first thing to catch its early morning rays was Cape Lookout Lighthouse, which towers 165 feet above the sand dunes of Carteret County. As it cast its shadow westward, it fell across a lovely strip of sand dotted with cedar, yaupon and sea myrtle. This was Shackleford Banks.

Here lived a sturdy race of people: the Guthries, Moores, Davises, Lewises, Chadwicks, Willises, Royals and Roses. With their bare hands they eked a meager living from the surf, oyster rocks and clam beds; and with their bare hands, they would attack and kill the world's largest living creature, the leviathan of the deep, the mighty whale.

This is how they did it, as related by an eyewitness, Captain Stacy Guthrie, whose father, Devine Guthrie, built the boats, and whose brother helped to kill the "Little Children." The sixty-five-foot mother, a right whale, was named because some of the older men had grown weary of waiting for a whale to show, and had gone off looking for clams and oysters. They had to use some "shirt-tail" boys to make up the crew. (All whales were given names.)

Lookouts were posted along the beach, and when a whale was sighted, they came running down the beach, shouting at the top of their voices, "Whale! Whale! Thar she blows!" At that moment pandemonium broke loose. Men, women and children came running from every direction, shouting, "Whale! Whale! Man the boats!" They grabbed hold of the three eighteen-foot whale boats and literally carried them into the surf, where eight men scrambled aboard each boat—six oarsmen, one helmsman in the stern and a harpoon man in the bow. These boats were made of wood lap-streak siding, oak and cedar ribs and knees, and were sharp at both ends. They were sturdy enough to stand severe pounding of the surf and an occasional slap of a whale's fluke.

Now the whales, when undisturbed, follow a set pattern. They blow (or come up to breathe) three times in a row at fifteen-minute intervals, and then they submerge for one hour. Therefore, Captain Guthrie was surprised when he saw the whale three times in less than five minutes, and gave a warning shout, "Look out boys! Thar's three whales out thar!" And to everyone's amazement, they discovered there was a bull, a mother and a calf.

The way of the sea is cruel indeed. The whalers had to first attack the calf, knowing that the bull would turn at the first sight of danger, but that the mother would stay and protect her baby, though it would cost her life. So they thrust a harpoon into the fleshy part of the calf, with no intent to kill it, as it had no cash value, but so they could get a better chance at the mother. Captain Stacy says that if you could injure a calf so badly that it can't rise for air, the mother will take it in her fluke and hold it above the water so it can breathe. When she knows it is dead, then she will head for the briny deep. In this case they did not kill the calf, but all three boats attacked the mother whale with the fury of desperate men, knowing that food for their babies depended on the death of this monster.

Captain Devine Guthrie. *Courtesy of the Carteret County History Society.*

To kill a whale, you have to hit its vital organs, which the whalers refer to as "her life." To do this, you aim about two feet under the water just aft of her spout. When she goes down, you follow by the whirlpools caused by her tail when she swims. A good boat crew can usually row as fast as she swims. When she rises and blows, they are there, ready for another thrust of the harpoon and a shot from the gun, which carries an explosive head. If the water is clear when she blows, you know you have missed the mark. If it is tinted with blood, you are getting close. If it is solid blood, you have hit "her life" and had better stay clear, for she then goes in her death struggle, slapping with her tail so hard it would smash your boat like a matchbox.

This time the men had down their work well. Slowly, the great beast began to calm down and the whirlpools and foaming waves subsided. Then, with one mighty last effort, she thrust herself half out of the water and then settled back beneath the surface. All the boats started closing in to where the whale had disappeared from view, and as they neared the spot, the great hulk rose slowly to the surface, motionless as a log. Then all the men stood up, held their oars straight up in the air and gave three loud whoops, telling the people anxiously watching along the shore that the battle was over and they had been victorious. That was also the signal for the women to head for home and "put on the pot."

At this point in the story, Captain Stacy was all fired up, but I just had to interrupt him with a question. I asked, "How come that whale to float? I thought all fish sank to the bottom when first killed." At that question, the fight went out of Captain Stacy's face and voice, and his eyes, which had been staring through the yaupons and cedars across the sand dunes far out into the ocean, shifted toward me and a smile lit up his face as he answered, "You know, Grayden, God had a lot to do with that. He marked it so there would be no mistake about who made it. He put 365 bones in its mouth for the days of the year; but the strangest thing of all is why a whale, as its life comes to an end, gradually turns toward the setting sun; but I know for sure that every whale killed along these shores died with its nose headed due sou'west."

To get this monster ashore was a herculean task. When the people on the beach got the signal that the whale was dead, Captain Devine Guthrie went out in a sailboat (sharpie) to give a hand. Three whale boats were fastened together and tied to the whale. They began to move it slowly toward the shore. When Captain Guthrie reached the scene, he fastened onto the lead boat and spread all the sails he had.

Nature smiled on those weary men, as a gentle breeze sprang up from the southwest and the tide started coming in. It was necessary to beach the whale when the tide was at its

Courtesy of Randy Newman, Fort Macon.

peak, so that when the tide went out, the men could wade out and start cutting away the thick outer flesh, or blubber, which has a very high oil content.

Before they started this tremendous job, all the men took a short nap and ate a hearty meal of "Conch Stew, Hard Crabs and Jumping Mullets." Now, "Conch Stew" to a Core Sounder is like spinach to Popeye. The men went about their task with superhuman strength.

They cut the blubber in chunks about eight by twelve inches, which the women and children toted ashore in washtubs and dumped into large iron kettles of try pots. A roaring fire was already briskly burning under the kettles. It took thirty or forty people three to four days to finish the job. The most important part was cooking the oil just right. If it was cooked too fast, it would turn dark; if too slow, it would smell and spoil. Only the old and experienced hands could do this work.

Cutting the blubber. *Courtesy of Randy Newman, Fort Macon.*

The oil, when finished, was poured out in pork barrels and wooden vats to cool. A merchant came over from Beaufort, sampled it and made an offer. Then the oil was sealed in wooden barrels, hauled across Shackleford Banks with a yoke of oxen, loaded on sailboats and brought over to Beaufort, where the crew was paid on the average of $1,000 for the total products of the whale. This divided among thirty or forty men amounted to about $35 per man. The average kill along the Shackleford Banks was one or two whales per season. The money from the whales supplied these hardy families with gunpowder and shot for hunting ducks, geese and loons. These wild fowl, with conchs, crabs, fish, oysters and scallops, along with collard, sweet potatoes and corn from their garden patch, made a satisfactory diet for them.

All in all, life was good. The sea was cruel, yet gave these hardy souls an adventurous, stimulating living. Some of the whalers went up north and fished for whale on regular whaling ships, as described in the following sea chanty.

∽

*boatswain—pronounced bo's'n *larboard—the left side of a ship
*overhaul—examine thoroughly *resolute—determined; firm; steady

THE WHALE SONG

The boatswain* on a mast so high
With a spy-glass in his hand;
"Thar a Whale! Thar's a Whale
Thar's a Whaley Fish!" he cried;
"Thar she blows off the larboard* stand, brave boys;
Thar she blows of the larboard stand."

The Captain on the quarter deck,
Such a brave young man was he:
"Overhaul! Overhaul!*
Let your davit take a fall.
And low'r your boats at sea, brave boys,
And low'r your boats at sea."

The boats being lowered and the crew got in.
The whale disappeared from view.
"Resolute! Resolute!"* To the whole boat's crew.
"And steer to where the Whale Fish blew, brave boys.
And steer to where the Whale Fish blew."

The Whale being struck and the line played out.
The fish gave a blow with his tail.
He capsized the boat and they lost six men;
"But neither did you kill that whale, brave boys,
But neither did you kill that Whale."

Oh, Greenland is an ice place.
There's never grass nor green.
Where ice and snow are always there
And daylight seldom seen, brave boys,
And daylight's seldom seen.

THE LOON HUNT

The people on Harkers Island still like to hunt loons, as proven by the following story.

The loon is a large, migratory waterfowl, just a little smaller than a goose. It has powerful, straight, hollow legs, and can outswim most any fish. Like its Southern competitor, the pelican, it eats its own weight in fish every day. It nests in Canada, but its favorite fishing ground is around Cape Lookout, North Carolina.

Near Cape Lookout, on Harkers Island, lives a hardy group of fisherfolk who would rather have a "loon in the pot" than the more popular goose, canvasback or redhead duck. They like to hunt the loon for three reasons. First, they like to eat it. Second, they use the leg bones for fishing lures. Third, the excitement of the forbidden hunt adds zest to the sport, which has been a part of their lives since their earliest days on the island. It is against the law to shoot the loon, and there is never an open season on hunting them. The United States has an international treaty with Canada for the controlled right to collect the loons' eggs for making glue.

One of the most avid loon hunters I ever knew was Telford Willis of Harkers Island. Many years ago, I would go to haul his fishing boat out on my railways in Beaufort several times a year. Every time he came to have this work done, he would excitedly tell me about his last loon hunt.

"Grayden," he would say, "You can stand there and shoot until your gun barrel gets so hot you have to lay it down to let it cool off."

A little bothered, I asked, "Telford, why in the world do you want to kill so many loons?"

He quickly answered, "That's just it. You don't kill 'um, you just shoot 'um."

I smugly said, "I'll bet you I can kill one every time I shoot."

"All right, come on down," he said, "and try your luck."

So I made plans and went down one morning before daylight. Telford was waiting at the appointed place. As I walked onto the dock, I saw ten other fellows in the boat. There were all hollering, "Come on, Grayden, hurry up! We got to get there before sunup."

We got in the boat and headed across the channel, about two miles from Harkers Island to Shackleford Banks. (Shackleford runs due west from Cape Lookout to Beaufort Inlet, a distance of eight miles.) We pulled the boat up on the sound side of the island and walked about a mile to the ocean side.

Here Telford and I stopped behind a big sand dune. The other fellows began to disappear in the semidarkness as they walked down the beach. When they thought they were out of gunshot reach of us, one of them stopped behind another sand dune. The others went on until they had spread out about a mile down the beach.

A little puzzled, I said, "Telford, I've been on a lot of hunting trips, but this beats all I've ever seen." Telford whispered, "You just be patient. The loons will start flying any time now, and you'll see."

Loons don't fly in flocks like most other waterfowl. They usually fly alone or in pairs. They fly just offshore of the breakers, parallel with the beach, but farther offshore and flying faster than you think. Just about the first flutter of dawn I heard a gun fire way up the beach. Telford was getting excited, and said, "Get down, Grayden; here he comes!" About that time another gun went off, and I saw a loon coming, seemingly about six feet above the water and about six hundred yards away. "Bang!" went another gun, and I saw some feathers fly off the loon, but he kept right on coming. That loon flew the gauntlet of ten sand dunes, guns booming and feathers flying, until he got right abreast of our sand dune. Telford gave me a nudge and said, "All right, Grayden, here's your chance. Stand up and let him have it."

I stood up and held that thirty-two-inch Long Tom about two feet ahead of the loon's bill and cut loose both barrels. Telford emptied his five-shot automatic in the same direction. What few feathers were left flew off, but the loon kept right on going. Telford threw his gun down in disgust and doubled up his fist. He shook it at the disappearing loon and shouted, "Go it! You straight leg. We may not eat you, but you'll freeze to death this winter."

THE SHIP THAT
NEVER RETURNED

Those who lived on Harkers Island were not only whalers and hunters, but were also good boat builders, and they had a natural supply of material for the job, as Shackleford Banks abounded in cedar and pine. The cedar limbs grew in just the right shape to make the "knees," or frames, for the boats. However, the islanders soon discovered that because of the prevalence of hurricanes and pirates the Outer Banks were no place for a permanent shipbuilding business. So, in 1825, they moved their business over to Beaufort and were encouraged and financially helped by prominant businessmen such as the Bordens, Stantons, Hellens and Otway Burns. They built many fast clipper ships that sailed the seven seas, as well as the first steamboat that ran from Wilmington to Fayetteville up the Cape Fear River.

In the year 1848, gold was discovered in California, and everybody started west by covered wagon, mule back or by foot, and some started by water. One of these was a big landowner and a stockholder in the Beaufort Ship Building Company, Penn Hellen, the great-great-great-uncle of Wiley Taylor Jr. He sold a block of his property in Beaufort (the post office square) for $600, formed a company, built three ships and started out for California. The Panama Canal had not yet been built, so he had to sail around Cape Horn, the most treacherous water passage in the world, where two of his ships were lost with all their crew members.

One of those ships did get to California, and they did strike gold. Some of the old houses still standing in Beaufort today were built with that gold. Captain Penn Hellen and his ship were lost rounding the Horn on their return trip.

Some such tragedy inspired someone to write a song called "The Ship That Never Returned."

THE SHIP THAT NEVER RETURNED

(first stanza)
On one summer day when the waves were rippling
With a cool, soft gentle breeze,
Did a ship set sail with her cargo laden
For a port beyond the seas.

(chorus)
Did she ever return? No, she never returned,
And her fate is yet unlearned;
So for years and years there were loved ones watching
For the ship that never returned.

(second stanza)
"Only one more trip," said the gallant captain,
As he kissed his weeping wife.
"Only one more bag of this golden treasure
That will last us all through life."

(third stanza)
"Then we'll settle down in our cozy cottage,
And enjoy the rest we've earned."
But alas! Poor man, he sailed commander,
On the ship that never returned.

THE WRECK OF THE
CRISSIE WRIGHT

The mural hanging in the post office in Beaufort depicts the eight-hundred-ton, three-masted schooner *Crissie Wright*, which fetched up and foundered on January 11, 1886, abreast the Banker village of Wades Shore Shackleford Banks, with the loss of all hands except the ship's cook. Could you have stood at noontime on that date at the front door of this post office, you would have seen the tops of the masts of this vessel above the woods of Shackleford Banks. Even today, on an extremely low tide, you can see the keel and ribs protruding through the sand.

There have been many ships wrecked along the shores of North Carolina since Ralph Lane, the English explorer, first landed at Cape Lookout in 1585; but the tragic story of the *Crissie Wright* has lingered longest in the minds of the residents of Carteret County, and has been kept alive by the colloquialism that, even now, almost a hundred years later, you will hear whenever the temperature dips below twenty degrees: "It's gonna get colder than the time the *Crissie Wright* went ashore."

This beautiful three-masted schooner was eighty-four days out of Rio de Janeiro, headed for its home port of New York with a full cargo of phosphates. As it passed Cape Fear and headed north along the North Carolina coast, it was making good time, with a stiff sou'wester and the Gulf Stream both in its favor. The crew began to dream of the happy reunion with their families and the bonus pay they would get for delivering their cargo safely to New York. However, destiny was about to change their luck.

As they approached Cape Lookout, Captain Zeb Collins, with his "weather eyes" peeled, noticed a dark cloud forming in the northeast, and called the crew together for consultation. Aboard the *Crissie Wright*, in addition to the captain, were First Mate John C. Blackman, Second Mate Samuel E. Grover, Carpenter James Boswell, Seaman Samuel Dosier, Ship's Cook Robert Johnson and Cabin Boy Chester Simmons. The weather was already getting blustery and they knew a shift was in the offing.

Diamond Shoals off Cape Hatteras had already become known as "the Graveyard of the Atlantic," so Captain Collins, being a prudent sailor, decided to take shelter in Cape Lookout bight. They were then about five miles offshore, east of Cape Lookout, so they made a larboard tack and stood in toward the beach.

As they approached the hook of the cape, the wind was about to shift and was baffling when suddenly the sails were caught aback, and this parted the main brace. The ship would not answer the helm and was unmanageable. It paid off and would not come about. There was nothing for the crew to do but to heave to and shorten the sail.

To keep from going immediately on the beach, they anchored. The weather conditions became more boisterous, and the sea became very rough. By taking bearings on objects ashore, the captain realized that he was dragging anchor and was slowly being driven ashore by the screaming gale. There was nothing they could do but watch their ship approach the outer break, which was about two hundred yards from the beach.

Crissie Wright came ashore stern first, and the crew felt their ship grind into the outer reef. Its bow slowly fell off the larboard until it was breached larboard side to, with every sea breaching it from stern to stern.

What a plight for a ship to be in! Broached side to, stove and taking water faster than any pumps could ever drain it. The only alternative that Captain Collins had was to give the order for the crew to lie aloft on the foremast shroud and lash themselves to the ratlines. That evening the wind veered to northwest and freshened to full gale force, and the temperature dropped to eight degrees Fahrenheit during the night. Those poor crew members, soaking wet and lashed to the rigging on that heavy mast with that gale sucking the breath out of their lungs—what could have been a worse predicament for human beings to be in? Imagine the sight that greeted the eyes of those people there ashore—seven men silhouetted against the red sky of dawn. They were slowly freezing to death with no help available, even though they were within sight of a roaring fire on the beach and the people there. It would have been very foolhardy to have attempted to launch a dory in the raging surf.

That day Captain Collins simply froze to death and fell from aloft into the boiling sea, never to be seen again. Mr. Blackman and Seaman Dosier were swept overboard to instant death while attempting to get forward to the forecastle. Somehow the second mate, carpenter, cook and cabin boy managed to get under protection of the jib boom and wrapped themselves in the stay sail and jib.

While this tragedy was going on, about half of the population of Diamond City had gathered on the shore to watch as Captain Seef Willis, John Lewis and their whaling crews tried in vain to launch their whaleboats in the face of ten-foot waves and go to the rescue. But darkness fell, with no hope in sight of saving the crew, so the whalemen built a big bonfire and waited for the coming of dawn. During the night, the wind and the waves subsided. With the first ray of light, they launched their boats and headed for the wreck. As they neared the ship, the saw no signs of life. After boarding, they saw a big bugle in the jib sail, and discovered four men wrapped together in the sail. They were all frozen still, but the man underneath, covered by the other three, showed some signs of life. This was the ship's cook, Robert Johnson.

They brought all the bodies ashore and thawed Johnson out slowly by the fire. Later, the bodies were all brought to Beaufort, and Johnson was sent to the Naval Hospital at Charleston, South Carolina, where he recovered somewhat

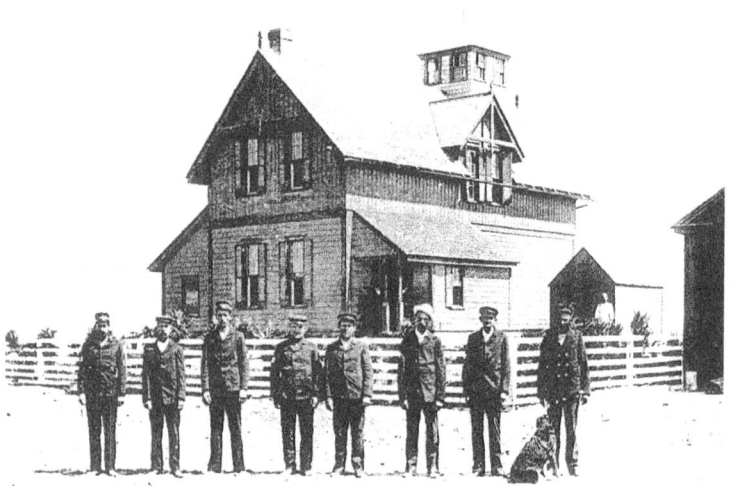

Lifesaving station. *Courtesy of the North Carolina Maritime Museum.*

physically, but never mentally. He died a year later. The other three were buried in a common grave in the old burying ground in Beaufort. Mr. Sam Darling, now dead, was a ten-year-old boy at the time, and just before he died, he told me that he stood there, holding his mother's hand, and watched his townspeople dig a hole, in which they placed the three bodies. This unmarked spot is near Purvis Chapel, and near the grave where the English sailor is buried standing up.

This wreck hastened the decision of the government to build lifesaving stations along the North Carolina coast—and many brave men have lost their lives in an effort to save others. The following song tells the story of one of these brave men and his children.

❧

THE COAST GUARDSMAN'S CHILDREN

Two little children, a boy and a girl,
Sat by the old church door.
The little girl's cheeks were as brown as the curls,
That hung on the dress that she wore.

The boy's coat was faded, and hatless, his head,
A tear shone in each little eye.
"Why don't you run home to your mother?" I said
And this was the maiden's reply.

"Mamma got sick. Angels took her away.
Left Jim and me all alone.
We come here to stay 'til the close of the day,
For we have no Mamma or home."

"Daddy was lost out at sea long ago;
We waited all night on the shore.
For he was a life-saving Captain, you know,
And never came back any more."

The Sexton came early to ring the Church bell;
He found them beneath the snow white.
The Angels made room for the orphans to dwell
In Heaven with Mamma that night.

Their Mamma's in Heaven, God took her away,
Left Jim and his sister alone.
They came here to stay, 'til the close of the day,
For they had no Mamma or home.

THE DAVIS SHORE
FREEZE

It was the year 1898, the coldest year ever recorded by the weather bureau in Carteret up to that time. It was also a year of famine, and a lot of people were hungry. It was especially hard for people who lived in isolated communities like Davis, which lies on the west side of Core Sound about twenty miles east of Beaufort and is completely surrounded by water.

Here lived a very hardy and self-reliant people, among whom were my father and grandfather. They grew their own corn, potatoes, pork, beef and vegetables. They had access to seafood and wildfowl—that is, in normal times. But this was a long, cold winter, and a depression had been on for years. Their food supply soon ran out, and they had to depend entirely on what they could catch from the water. But to add to their dismay, a terrible freeze came, and all the sounds and bays were frozen solid, so they could get no more food from the water. Many people got sick from starvation, and some died; but the cold weather stayed on, until finally Core Sound was frozen all the way to the Banks.

There was a group of colored folks who lived nearby at the Ridge. The leader of their clan was "Uncle Mose" Davis. It was he who suggested to the folks on Davis that they'd better have a prayer meeting. So all able-bodied men and women gathered down on the shore at Oyster Creek and Uncle Mose was the first one to pray. They all bowed their heads and he said, "O lord, we've gathered here to ask you to help us out of our troubles. We've done everything we can for ourselves, and unless you do something to help us, we are all gonna starve to death. Amen."

Then, before anybody else could start praying, somebody said, "Look over the Banks. What is that I see?" Somebody said, "That's a cloud." "No," said somebody else, "That's smoke I see. A spiral leading up from the beach. That must be somebody signaling for help." "How in the world can we help them?" somebody asked. "You can't get a boat over there, and no fool is going to walk out on that ice. Why, you would break through and freeze to death." Uncle Mose broke in and said, "Fellows, you ought to be ashamed of yourselves. We came here to ask God to help us, and we're not willing to help somebody else."

So they took a twenty-foot skiff lying close by, tied three lines to the bow and three men tied the lines around their waists and stepped out on the ice, pulling the skiff behind them. If the ice did break, they could pull themselves back into the boat. They soon discovered that the ice was thick enough to hold them, so they made their way slowly three miles across Core Sound to Core Banks, from where the smoke signals were still coming. When they reached the top of the sand hills, they saw a group of men sitting around the fire. Then they saw a ship wrecked on the shoals, just offshore. Do you know what that ship was loaded with? Molasses and grain, which saved the people of Davis Shore from starving to death.

Was this an answer to their prayer? Those people on Davis Shore thought so. The ship's name was *Pontiac*. Some of the furnishings from the captain's cabin are in the home of the late Elmo Wade, of Williston.

OTWAY BURNS

B efore the War of 1812, Otway Burns was in command of a merchantman sailing from New Bern to Portland, Maine. When he heard that war had been declared, he carried his vessel to New York, changed its name to *Snap Dragon* and had it equipped as a ship of war. It was a vessel of 147 tons, and when first fitted out carried a crew of seventy-five men, with armament of five carriage guns, fifty muskets and four blunderbusses. It was a beautiful ship, and so swift it could walk the water like a thing of life. Burns opened books of subscription in New Bern to capital stock. Contrary to public opinion, privateering was legal and he had to fight a few times to make this convincing to a number of people.

For two and a half years, beginning in 1812, Burns traveled the ocean from Newfoundland to the northern coast of South America, near the equator, capturing ships when feasible, placing prize crews on them and then sending them into ports with their riches. When this was not possible, he relieved the enemy ships of their cargo and burned the vessels.

During his first seven months at sea, Burns captured two barks, five brigs, three schooners and their cargoes valued at $1 million, and captured 250 prisoners. He met danger always from the enemy, and he was crippled many times by storms, but he always said, "If a vessel could scud nine knots an hour, no sea could board her."

In 1814, Burns sailed with Decokely as his lieutenant. He was putting into Beaufort Harbor for repairs when he saw a strange ship pretending to be poling. He happened to know that the water there was seven fathoms deep, so he drew near to investigate. He found old friends and acquaintances aboard the vessel, which delighted all his temporarily homesick crew. He then sailed into Beaufort for necessary repairs.

When the *Snap Dragon* made its last cruise, Burns was laid up in Beaufort with rheumatism, brought on by great exposure to all kinds of weather at sea. Reluctantly, he told Lieutenant Decokely goodbye. Decokely set sail, enthusiastically resolved to renew the fight with the enemy.

The British had determined to rid the seas of the *Snap Dragon*, so they prepared a special man-of-war, named the *Leopard*, to fight Burns's ship to the bitter end. They carried concealed guns, and the ship was disguised to look like a merchantman. Lieutenant Decokely fell into the snare. The *Snap Dragon* was running close to the *Leopard*, feeling perfectly safe, when the *Leopard* opened its broadside upon Lieutenant Decokely. The *Snap Dragon* fought with old-time courage, but when Commander Decokely and others lay dead on deck, with many others wounded, the *Snap Dragon*'s flag was lowered to the enemy for the first time in all its career. The ship was carried to England, and the crew was sent to Dartmoor prison.

It is told, but not as documented fact, that some of the crew of the *Snap Dragon* were taken from the Dartmoor prison and were forced to sail on the ship *Bounty*. They burned the ship, built homes on Pitcairn, married from the island and reared families.

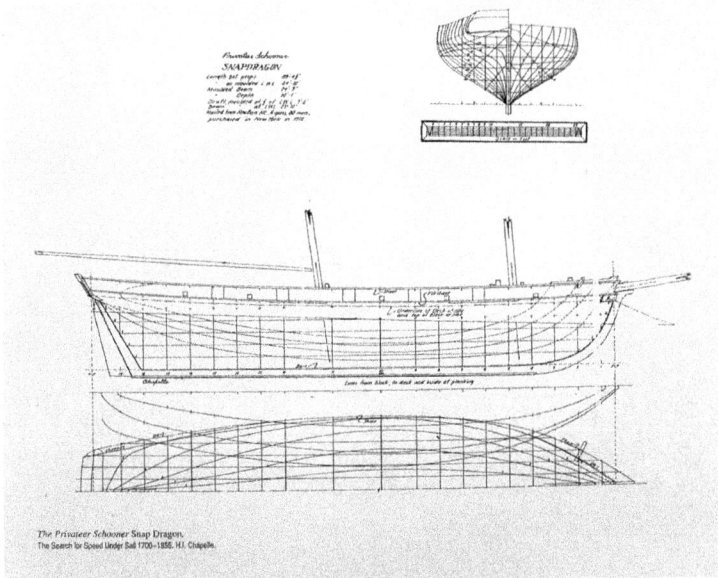

Loft lines for the privateer schooner *Snap Dragon*. *Courtesy of the North Carolina Maritime Museum.*

Otway Burns's grave is in the Beaufort Cemetery, and an imposing tombstone has been erected over the grave by his grandsons. A small town in Cateret County was named Otway in honor of Otway Burns, as well as the town Burnsville in Yancey County, North Carolina.

THE HAMMOCK HOUSE

Many stories have been told about the house in Beaufort, North Carolina, now known as the Hammock House. Some of these have basis in fact; some have gathered color and momentum in the telling. All the tales have added mystery and fascination to the history of this old house. No doubt, this house has seen its share of tragedy, love, happiness, sickness and the ebb and flow of life and death. If this building could talk, many questions could be answered that so tantalize the imagination today. Why was this house built? Was it for a pioneer family with children, a rendezvous for sailors or traders, a gentleman of wealth seeking retirement in isolation or for pirates who sought a place of refuge from their enemies and storms? We do not know. This old house keeps its secrets well, but out of the dim past, a few facts have been deduced.

We have heard that the ten- by ten-inch heart pine sleepers of the house, still in good repair, were stamped 1700, and that many people in Beaufort saw this date when the sleepers of the deserted house were exposed at one time. Deeds for land and property in America in the early days were hard to obtain. Any person who paid his own way to the colonies, settled on land, made improvements and assumed other obligations was given a grant consisting of from fifty to one hundred acres of land. This was called the headright system. This system was used up until 1730, when it was discontinued. The property for the Hammock House may have been obtained in this manner, or the land may have been taken over by someone and claimed as his own. These facts complicated research for first titles.

Since sawmills were in existence here about 1700, according to Lefler and Newsome's *North Carolina History*, the lumber for the Hammock House may have been sawed from native timber, although the timbers in the attic of the house are definitely hand hewn. Alternately, the timbers may have been taken by pirates from transport ships for the purpose of building this house. When the Hammock House was built, Beaufort was a struggling settlement, not an incorporated town, not even laid off in lots; and this isolated location could have befriended the unscrupulous. The two-story structure of the Hammock House, indeed, must have looked like a mansion to those pioneers who happened to see it. The house, nestled in groves of water oak, cedars, yaupon and chinquapin trees, towered on a hillock twelve feet above sea level. The banks down to the water were covered with wild grapes, tangled vines and sea myrtle. A dirt road led to the back of the house from the settlement that was to become Beaufort, but actually, the road was no more than a glorified path. There is little record, however, that the first owners had much contact with the settlement. Boats were tied to the columns of the house during high tide, and boats were used for transportation, perhaps more than any other means of travel.

The land must have been very fertile, because old records attest to vegetable and flower gardens as well as grapevines that flourished. A natural spring furnished pure water for the tenants, and the remains of a very old well are still on the premises.

Hammock House sketch. *Courtesy of the Beaufort Historical Association.*

It seems that the Coree and Tuscarora Indian uprising of 1712 left the Hammock House untouched. The house may have been used by pirates about this time, as they were raiding this part of the coast from 1689 to 1718, and such a desirable location as this house would not have gone unnoticed by these marauders.

Mr. Leslie Davis, a lawyer, deceased, said he found a deed claiming that Thomas Austin sold the Hammock House in 1719, but as yet we have not found this deed and date documented. There is every reason to believe this patent existed, because in our research, time and again, Thomas Austin's name is mentioned as having owned the Hammock House before 1719. For instance, in Book C of a town deed dated November 11, 1719, a transfer of property from Richard Rustell to Nathaniel Taylor reads, "To ye eastward of ye Hammock Place that Thomas

Austin formerly lived on." When the Cateret County Courthouse was destroyed by fire, some of the saved records were carried to New Bern and some to Raleigh; so research of this kind is very time consuming and requires great patience.

Before 1719, there is little known as fact about the house. In 1725, Nathaniel Taylor purchased the house, and on Moseley's map of 1733, the house was shown as the Taylor House, the first name given the house as far as is known. We know also that when Tryon Palace was first constructed in New Bern in 1769, the Hammock House was an old house even then. It seems, too, that the creek that bathed the shores of the property was originally called Beaver Creek and later Town Creek; but after Taylor's purchase of the house the creek became known as Taylor's Creek. Old deeds also speak of the island across the creek as Cart Island, the island we now know as Carrot Island.

After Nathaniel Taylor's purchase of the house in 1725, we find from old records of owners many interesting names that even now are familiar to us: Austin, Bell, Whorton, Mosley, Cooke (of the ram ironclad *Albemarle* fame), Liggett (later of Liggett and Myers fame), Foro (an outstanding merchant of New York), Mace (even Borden Mace), Fulford, Mason, Carraway, Piver, Simpson, Owens, Chadwick, Gibbs, Leffers, Davis, Martin, Pinder, Rustull and so on. All of these people owned the property at some time, though they did not necessarily all live in the house.

The Hammock House has had many names. The first name, as far as we know, was the Taylor House, and then the White House. This latter name appeared on maps as early as 1738, and the house was designated as an official marker for ships entering Beaufort Harbor. Then it was called Cook's Hammock. Later it was called the Mason House. Since 1875 it has been called the Hammock, or Hummock, House.

Hammock House. *Courtesy of the Beaufort Historical Association.*

Here are some interesting advertisements found in old newspapers. Note that all these dates were before the Civil War. As a digression, New Bern had a newspaper as early as 1751, the *N.C. Gazette*, published by James Davis, supposedly the father of the James Davis who built Mr. Joe House's house, the Longest House, Dr. Costlow's house and others in Beaufort.

Appearing in the *New Bernian* in 1843:

> *For Sale—A desirable summer residence, a good two story dwelling with outhouses, 42 acres of land called, "Cook's Hammock," situated on Taylor's Creek, adjoining Beaufort. For term, apply "Borden Mace."*

June 10, 1857 *Beaufort Journal*:

> *For Sale—Residence known as Hammock House—*
> *Office on Turner Street next to W.H. Piver's store.*
> *Several acres of ground, large, commodious dwelling,*
> *necessary outhouses, two gardens, spring of water. All in*
> *good condition.*
>
> Dr. J.B. Outlaw, New Bern, N.C.

The Civil War was nearing, money was getting scarce and Dr. Outlaw was becoming impatient to sell after over two years of ownership, as seen in the *Beaufort Journal* of June 17, 1859:

> *Residence for Sale—Hammock House—One of the*
> *most delightful residences to be found on sea coast.*
> *Comprises several acres of land with a large and*
> *commodious dwelling, and every necessary outhouse.*
> *Two good and large gardens, excellent spring of water*
> *all in good repair.*
>
> *Particulars deemed unnecessary as all who wish to*
> *purchase would examine for themselves, and are referred*
> *to J.S. Pender, Esq. of the "Atlantic House," Beaufort,*
> *who will show them the premises and give them any*
> *desired information.*
>
> Dr. J.B. Outlaw

Mr. Charles Norcom, now deceased, previously a general foreman for the Fuller Construction Company of Washington, D.C., and New York, went with me in 1961 to examine the Hammock House in order to give me expert, detailed information about the construction of the house and to verify the original material remaining.

The house is of Bahamas-style architecture. Trade was carried on with the Bahamas as early as 1640. Edward Teach (more commonly known as Blackbeard) and other pirates made their stronghold there. These pirates and traders came into Beaufort Harbor from the Bahamas. Consequently, the architecture found in the Bahamas had its influence on buildings in Beaufort. The Hammock House faces south on Taylor's Creek. All the land now lying between the Hammock House and Taylor's Creek has been pumped in. The waters of the creek at one time beat against the hillock on which the house stands.

The house rests on a foundation of stones that were used as ballast on sailing vessels. It was constructed of heart pine, lap-side weather boarding, seven inches to the weather. Most of the original boards are still on the house. These boards are still in perfect condition, and in places the original plaster made from oysters' shells is still on some of the walls. One roof covers the house and upstairs porch. There are two stories with eight rooms. The large attic has livable space. Originally an ell extended from the house to the east, and housed the kitchen. Two large chimneys of stone, six feet by four feet by thirty inches deep, with tops shaped like Turkington Balsam bottles, flank the east and west sides of the house and furnish fireplaces for the upstairs and downstairs rooms. The mantels over the fireplaces are the ones that were used when the house was first built. The colonial columns of eight inches in diameter, which support the porches, were put on with dowels; with the exception of one, they are the original columns.

The front door is thirty inches off center, and the stationary glass transom seems to be the original. Two original doors, with agate-colored knobs and the original hand-wrought black iron hinges, are still in use in the upstairs rooms. The upstairs original door casings are still in good repair.

The original window frames still on the house are made of oak. Handmade nails, forged on an anvil, were used in construction. The windows have nine panes in the upper sash and six panes in the lower sash, but they have no weights.

The attic has four-inch heart pine exposed rafters, which are hand hewn, mortised, tenoned at the ridge pole and put together with wooden dowels. The attic floor has the original six-inch pine flooring.

There were stables at one time for taking care of at least four horses and a coach, and necessary outhouses were on the premises. These were destroyed by fire long ago.

For many years, even in the lifetime of some of Beaufort's older citizens, the Hammock House was looked upon as a place of mystery. Its original beginnings were spoken of with bated breath, and parents warned their children, "Don't go near the Hammock House!" Mrs. Mary Arrington (Miss Lessie's mother) told me that many times when she was a girl, her parents brought her in by oxcart from the Gibbs farm to get their corn ground at the Hammock House. There was a windmill there in the late 1800s, known to have been in existence as early as 1795.

During the Civil War, the Confederate troops were encamped on the ground where Beaufort's new cemetery is located. A family lived in the Hammock House, where they enjoyed many of the things that were difficult to get during the war. The mistress of the house had molasses and some sugar for preserving. Perhaps the head of the house was a sea captain who could bring the molasses and sugar from the Bahamas. The lady grew many fruits and vegetables on the then-fertile soil around the Hammock House. Her young daughter was the proud possessor of a pony. The mother packed a basket of the good things she had preserved and baked, and the daughter rode the pony, carrying the basket, to the sick soldiers encamped on the present cemetery site.

In the very beginning of the life of the Hammock House, the stories related were not so worthy. It was told that many "carryings-on" took place there. Because of its isolation, strange things took place. The owner, a sea captain, perhaps a pirate, had a beautiful wife whose virtue was not as lovely as her face. Wearying of being alone, she sent for gay friends, who arrived by coach. They were installed in the house while the husband was at sea, and husband and faithfulness were forgotten. One night, the suspicious husband returned home secretly by small boat. He challenged his wife's lover to a duel. Instead, a terrible fight took place. The husband chased his wife's lover up the attic steps and killed him. The bloodstains are supposed to still be visible on the attic floor. Other stories say these stains are a result of sheep being slaughtered there in very cold weather. The Hammock House is definitely supposed to be haunted.

For many years when the house stood idle, even adults would not go near the place after dark. Even so, the house's enduring materials, sill of the builders and resistance to storms for at least 250 years or more have made it a treasure that awes even the cynic who believes only what he sees. It must have been such a house as the Hammock House that inspired Oliver Goldsmith to write:

> *Vain transitory splendor! Could not all*
> *Reprieve the tottering mansion from its fall?*
> *Obscure, it sinks: nor shall it more impart*
> *An hour's importance to the poor's man heart.*

FAITH AND CHARITY

Back in 1823, a Mr. Langdon and his family lived in Beaufort in a house on the southwest corner of Craven and Ann Streets across from the Methodist church. This house still stands and is now the home of Miss Lucile Rice. Langdon had attractive identical twin daughters named Faith and Charity. Their mother often dressed the young girls in blue dresses with blue-checked pinafores, and they were fondly known in town as the "two little girls in blue."

Although it was difficult to distinguish between them, as far as looks were concerned, they had very different personalities. Faith was fun loving, mischievous, gay and inclined to be a little selfish. She enjoyed confusing even her friends about which twin was which. Sometimes her pranks would involve stern measures on the part of her parents. Charity was very shy, but her adoration of her sister influenced her to go along with her pranks, and she enjoyed the caprices of Faith since, in her estimate, Faith could do no wrong.

Mr. Langdon, father of the twins, was a merchant and bought his merchandise from wares brought into the harbor by sailing schooners hailing from Northern cities and sometimes abroad. One day a handsome young captain

Langdon House. *Courtesy of the Beaufort Historical Association.*

sailed into Beaufort Harbor. He had business dealing with Mr. Langdon and Mr. Langdon cordially invited the captain to stay as a guest in his home. There he met the two sisters, Faith and Charity.

After a lengthy stay, the captain found he had fallen in love with the shy sister, who so graciously had helped her mother with household duties and had made his stay in their home so comfortable. The day of departure came and reluctantly the young captain sailed away. He declared his love by letter and proposed marriage to the frail, timid sister, but confused the names of the sisters. Sad to say, he addressed his letters to Faith instead of Charity, the sister he really loved. Faith answered his letters and accepted his proposal of marriage.

She told some of her friends about her love, and soon it was known in the town that she would marry her captain someday. Her trousseau was prepared, and Charity, with an aching heart, but with love for her sister, spent hours sewing the precious linens that were to go in Faith's hope chest.

Again, after many weeks, the young captain sailed into Beaufort to claim his bride. Crossing Beaufort Bar, the seas were rough, and the captain lost most of his cargo. When he landed, the rain and wind beat upon the town as if resisting his intrusion. He arrived at the home of his prospective bride with a fast-beating heart, although his spirits were somewhat dampened by the bad weather and the loss of most of his cargo. Much to his surprise, he was greeted at the door by Faith, who threw her arms around him with great fervor.

The young captain, realizing this was the wrong maiden, sought the father in private as soon as he tactfully could. "Sir," he said, "this is a dismal day for me. Something has gone wrong as I found when I arrived in your home. The weather seems to be against me, and things seem to have been mixed up here. I believe Providence is even unfavorable toward me."

Hurriedly, the father replied, "My dear young man, you must not speak that way. My son, just have Faith." "That's just it, Sir," said the captain. "I don't want Faith—I want Charity."

This alarmed the father, who knew of the preparation that Faith, his wife and even the unselfish Charity had made. Why, the whole town thought Faith was to be married!

Since Charity had never revealed her secret love for the captain, the father insisted that the captain marry Faith and spare her from the pain of what she would have to face if the marriage did not take place. So the captain and Faith were married.

But poor Charity! She retired into seclusion, never again leaving her home. Beaufort people said they never saw her on the streets again. It was also said she died about a year later of a broken heart, but actually it was tuberculosis that took her life.

Two Little Girls in Blue

(first stanza)
Come listen my lad to a story I'll tell,
A story that's strange but true.
Your Daddy and I at school one day
Met two little girls in blue.

(chorus)
Two little girls in blue, lad,
Two little girls in blue.
They were sisters, and we were brothers
And learned to love them true.
One little girl in blue, lad
Did win your father's heart.
Became your mother, I married the other;
But we have drifted apart.

(second stanza)
The picture of one of those girls my lad,
To me she was once a wife.
I found her unfaithful, we quarreled, lad,
And parted that night for life.

BURIED TREASURE

Many tales are told of buried pirate treasure along the coast—some true, some false. This is a true story about an enterprising Yankee sergeant during the Battle of Fort Macon in the year 1862.

When North Carolina seceded from the Union in 1861, Captain Josiah Pender (who is rests in the old burying ground near the Baptist church) led a company of fifty men who took the fort from a small, unsuspecting group of Federals, and held it for one year and eleven days, until it was retaken by General Ambrose E. Burnside in April 1862. The fort had been under siege by Federal gunboats for some time, but they were unable to take it because of the powerful guns that controlled the inlet and harbor.

After the fall of New Bern, the Federal land forces pushed on down toward Beaufort, encountering some resistance at Newport, but occupied Beaufort with a fight. General Burnside set up headquarters in the house on Queen Street now owned by Stanley Potter, and decided to make a land attack on the fort.

Knowing the fort was not defended from the land, since all the guns pointed toward the sea, he sent a group of artillerymen up Bogue Sound with instructions to build rafts, float their artillery pieces across the sound and attack the fort from the rear. When the rafts were all completed and loaded, the sergeant in charge of construction called all the men together and told them, "Gentlemen, we are going on a very dangerous mission, and we have been instructed not to let anything of value fall into the hands of the enemy; so I want you to bring me all your money and jewelry. We will bury it here on the banks of Bogue Sound. When the battle is over, we will return here and I will give you back your belongings."

So they selected a big cedar tree as the spot for burial, dug a hole at the root of the tree, buried the treasure right under the tree and left no sign of digging, but marked the tree so they could find it on their return. Then they floated their cannons across the sound and pulled them up to the proper position for firing on the fort.

Fort Macon in the Civil War. *Courtesy of Paul Branch, Fort Macon.*

Fort Macon aerial view. *Courtesy of Paul Branch, Fort Macon.*

As history records, it was a short battle. The fort soon surrendered, and the men were ordered back to Beaufort by boat and sent off to other battlegrounds. That is, all except the sergeant, who in some way managed to stay in Beaufort until the war was over.

He waited until he thought everybody had forgotten the affair and then he made a deal with a local fisherman, Mr. Gabriel. He told Mr. Gabriel that if he would take him in his boat to where the treasure was buried, he would give him half the treasure. So they got in Mr. Gabriel's dugout and started. Mr. Gabriel had to do all the rowing since the sergeant did not know anything about boats. About halfway there, Mr. Gabriel noticed that the sergeant was looking strange, so he said, "Man, are you sick?" He replied, "I sure am." Mr. Gabriel reached over, put his hand on his forehead and said, "You are burning up with fever. I better get you to a doctor." So they turned around and came back to Beaufort.

By the time they reached the foot of Orange Street, where Dr. Manney's office was located, the sergeant was unconscious. Mr. Gabriel carried him on his shoulders about a block to the office. As soon as Dr. Manney saw the sergeant, he knew the man had typhoid fever. The sergeant soon died, but never revealed his secret about the location of the treasure. Although many cedars in this section have been uprooted, the treasure has never been found.

WHEN THE BOOZE
YACHT RAN ASHORE

Back in the days of Prohibition, bootlegging was a big business. Whiskey was brought over from England and other countries in ships, but the bootleggers dared not come inside the three-mile limit of shore for fear of being sighted by the Coast Guard, so a thriving business sprang up known as rumrunning.

Around the United States ports, small boats would go out, get a load of whiskey and try to sneak into port, past the Coast Guard, under cover of darkness. Sometimes they got caught, and the cargo was confiscated and the crew put in jail. But in some cases the rumrunners had specially built boats with powerful engines that could outrun the Coast Guard boats. Such was the case of a yacht named the *Adventure*, which was intercepted at the Beaufort Bar, but turned tail and headed up the beach toward Cape Lookout, with the Coast Guard in pursuit. The boat soon outran the Coast Guard, and the rumrunners thought they had escaped; but about that time they hit shoal and stuck fast. So they threw the whiskey overboard to lighten the boat and did manage to escape. The next day, some fishermen from Harkers Island were making a haul for mullets and found several cases of whiskey in their net. The crew decided to keep it quiet and make another haul the next day; but one of their members drank a little too much and spread the news all over the island, so the bottles were soon all "caught."

The most famous gathering place back then was Cleveland Davis's general store and post office. In fact, it was such a busy place that the natives referred to it as the "Beehive."

The whiskey was in a bottle with a "King Lock" stopper, which old-timers will remember. It had a wire spring latch on it, which you pulled up to open, and you could reseal the bottle by pressing down on the latch.

At this time there was a man from New York living on Harkers Island by the name of Ralph Sanders. One of the popular tunes of the day was "The Sidewalks of New York." Sanders must have been somewhat of a composer, for he wrote a ballad called "The Booze Yacht" and sang it to the tune of his favorite song.

The late Ivey Scott, a famous fiddler, began playing and singing the song all over the county. It soon spread over the state, and Scott was invited to sing at many occasions far and wide. In fact, I received a letter shortly after Scott's death from the National Folklore Association of Philadelphia asking Ivey to come there and sing.

There may have been many verses to "The Booze Yacht," but the following are all I have been able to find.

THE BOOZE YACHT

(first stanza)
Down around the "Beehive," Harkers Island retreat,
Every night and morning the fishermen would meet.
One day there came a rounder; came running by the door,
"There's a Booze Yacht run ashore."

(chorus)
This way, that way, to the Cape they'd run.
The coming of the Booze Yacht, put fishing on the bum.
Some lost their religion and back-slid by the score,
And "King Lock" stoppers were stacked ace high
When the Booze Yacht run ashore.

(second stanza)
Things have changed since those times.
Some folks are up in "G."
Others, they are down and out, but most feel just like me.
Some would part with all they've got, and some a little more,
To see another time like that
When the Booze Yacht run ashore.

MR. FRISBY'S COW

M r. Frisby was a seafaring man who plied the coast from Boston to Charleston. Occasionally he stopped at Davis Shore to pick up a load of oyster shells and goose feathers. On one such trip, he met an attractive middle-aged woman, and they fell in love at first sight. He asked her to marry him, but she said she could not marry a seafaring man because she had lost her father and two brothers at sea, and had made up her mind not to lose a husband. However, if he would give up the way of the sea, she would marry him.

Captain Frisby said, "How could I ever make a living on land? I only know the sea." She said, "That is very simple. I will tell you how it is done. You get a breeding sow, some chickens and a milk cow, and you raise your own food." He said, "That sounds easy." So they got married and settled down in her old homeplace, a nice house with plenty of land. He sold his boat and bought the hogs, chickens and cow, as she suggested.

The cow had a calf and was producing lots of milk, so his wife said, "Come on, Mr. Frisby (she always called him Mr. Frisby until the day he died), and I will show you how to milk the cow." So they took the pail and a stool, and went out to the stall. Mr. Frisby was amazed at how easy it was to get the milk and said, "This is wonderful! Plenty of fresh milk all the time." But he had something to learn about cows. Soon the calf was weaned; the milk began to dry up. One morning Mr. Frisby went out as usual to get the milk but, to his surprise, no milk came.

He couldn't imagine what was wrong; so being used to bailing water out of boats, he thought of a plan to get the milk. He took a piece of rope, tied it around the cow's body at the forelegs, threw the rope over a rafter in the barn and began to take in the slack. Soon he had the cow standing on her hind feet, with her front feet dangling in the air.

About that time some of the neighbors came by. When they saw what was going on, they asked, "Mr. Frisby, what are you going to do, hang the cow?" "Why, no, "he said, "I am just trying to make the milk run aft."

Unknown Seas
(The Story of Nancy
Manney)

Early in the 1800s, a young man set out from Philadelphia for a land in the South that had intrigued his imagination even before he received his education. At last, with his new Doctor of Medicine diploma in his possession, he arrived in the beautiful city of New Bern. Such a gentleman as he was received graciously by the people there, and he was encouraged to start his practice of medicine. But his wish was to live nearer the ocean in a smaller town, where he felt the need for a doctor was vital.

Dr. Manney had fallen in love and married a young lady from New Bern. They decided that the small town of Beaufort, not far from New Bern, near the ocean, would be the ideal place to make their home. They were welcomed in Beaufort, and soon were established in the life of the community. Dr. Manney found his days busy with caring for the sick, and Mrs. Manney with the duties of a wife and mother. Eight children were born to the couple. The eldest was a son named James. The second child was a daughter named Nancy, who was born in 1820. It is about Nancy that our story is told.

With such a large family, Dr. Manney felt the need for someone to tutor the children. Mrs. Manney's health was none too good, and the task of the children's education was getting to be too much of a strain for her. Public schools were not of the best quality, if available, especially for girls and older children. Dr. Manney found a young man, Charles French, in Philadelphia, who he felt was qualified as tutor for the children. French soon arrived to begin his duties. Nancy at that time was sixteen years old, a beautiful young girl, a leader among her friends, loving life, talented and the pampered darling of her father.

After about two years, Charles French decided it was time for him to return to Philadelphia to continue his law studies, which had been interrupted during this time of tutoring. Many things had changed during these two years. Mrs. Manney had died, and Dr. Manney could not get over the shock and grief of his loss. He grew morose, and lost interest in things in general. His dependence on Nancy grew, and she assumed the responsibility for the younger children of the family.

Although Dr. Manney was adamant in his belief that slavery was wrong, he always had colored help in his home, but cared for them and paid them wages. The loyalty of some of these servants was a great help to Nancy during the later years, when misfortune overtook her. In the meantime, Nancy and Charles French had fallen in love, but thought they had kept this a secret. Dr. Manney sensed this situation and had built up a violent resentment and disfavor to this affair.

The time came for Charles French to leave. He approached Dr. Manney with the declaration of his love for Nancy, and asked permission to return as soon as his law studies were complete, to claim Nancy as his bride. Dr. Manney's reaction was one of anger, and in no uncertain terms he refused consent to an engagement between Nancy and Charles

French. Nonetheless, Charles French told Dr. Manney and Nancy that he would return some day and marry Nancy.

Nancy was heartbroken. This was the first thing her father had ever refused her. She was deeply in love and promised Charles she would wait for him, regardless of her father's disapproval. She told him she would pour out her love in her letters to him, and Charles promised he would also declare his love again and again in his letters to Nancy. He promised once more to return for her as soon as he became a lawyer and had a home for her.

Dr. Manney, seeing that both of the young people were determined to marry someday, began to take steps to stop the romance. During those days, the isolation of Beaufort, uncertainty of mail service, precariousness of travel and lack of government regulations regarding postal service made receiving letters unpredictable.

Dr. Manney, in his anger, grief and frustration, contacted the postmaster and bargained with him that the letters written by Charles French and Nancy should not reach their destinations. The agreement was made. No one knows just how or why.

After Charles French had gone, Nancy wrote to him, telling him of her love and recounting the day-to-day events in her life. Letters from Charles to Nancy were received at the post office, but the letters of both were tied together and stored in a special box with the postmaster's belongings. Neither Nancy nor Charles received a letter from the other. Dr. Manney died soon after this, never revealing his secret.

Nancy watched her sisters and brother, James, marry and leave her home, but she stayed on, refusing the attentions of other young men, waiting and longing for Charles's return. She continued to write him for a long time, keeping faith that someday he would come back to her. The War Between the States began. Nancy's finances were running low, and she had trouble even finding food and keeping her house in repair. Her brother, James, had become a doctor, and was stationed at Fort Macon for a while, and then practiced in Beaufort. Nancy, in her pride, refused his help and tried to carry her own load. Most of the slaves, in their new freedom, had started rioting and Beaufort streets were unsafe at night. James Manney tried to encourage Nancy to marry one of her suitors in Beaufort, but she refused, saying she had to be true to her only love, regardless. Since Charles French had not returned to her, she would marry no one else.

One day a messenger came to Nancy saying that the postmaster was very ill and was not expected to last through the night. He asked over and over to speak with Nancy. Nancy went to his home and he asked his servant to bring him a certain box. He gave the box to Nancy, asking her to open it. Inside she found the letters she and Charles had written to each other but never received. The postmaster told the story of what had taken place between himself and her father. The postmaster died that same day, after begging Nancy's forgiveness for the terrible thing he had done.

Nancy now knew nothing about Charles French, as his letters had stopped coming years before this, and resigned herself to the fact that Charles French had at last forgotten her. Nancy Manney at this time was about forty-five years old. The Civil War was at its peak, and Nancy busied herself with nursing the sick and wounded soldiers.

Time went by; the year was 1885. Once day the new postmaster sent for Nancy—what now? He told her that he had received a letter from a Mr. Charles French, lawyer, asking if he could give him any information about Nancy Manney or the Manney family. He said he would like to return to Beaufort if any of the family was still living there. Mr. Charles French had become chief justice of the Supreme Court of the Territory of Arizona. He had married there, but his wife had died a few years ago. His thoughts kept returning to the happy days he had spent in Beaufort and the girl he had always loved, Nancy Manney.

Nancy wrote to Charles French, begging him to return. The date was set, and Nancy was now about sixty-six years old. The years of struggle and unhappiness had taken their toll, but she awaited Charles's coming with a love that had lasted throughout all the years. Her health was failing and her tiny frail body was wracked with coughing. It seemed she could not last until Charles's ship could sail into Beaufort. Many of Nancy's friends assured her they would be on hand to welcome Charles French, since she was too ill to meet his ship. They filled her home with the red roses Charles had told her so long ago that she was like.

The reunion of these two was a bittersweet occasion, filled with regrets for the love that had been denied fulfilling for so long. Charles French persuaded Nancy that their remaining years, even days, should be spent together. Charles, an old man, a distinguished gentleman, knelt by Nancy's couch, took her in his arms and they were married.

Nancy died a few days after this, declaring her love for Charles and asking that no bitterness remain. These two had passed through those "unknown seas" at last—to reach harbor together.

BUS TOUR OF OLD BEAUFORT

L et's take a bus tour around the old streets of Beaufort. We will start on Ann Street, across from the old cemetery that was given to the town by Nathaniel Taylor in 1731. We notice the old elm trees that line the street. We also look through the gates of the cemetery from our bus and see the huge live oaks, the brilliant color of azaleas and the towering tombstones erected to loved ones of many years ago.

We turn the corner on Craven Street toward the north, and notice on the right a two-story house that was originally constructed before the Revolutionary War; but as tastes and time changed, the house was decorated with "gingerbread" trim. We also notice the tomb of Otway Burns mounted with the cannon from his ship, *Snap Dragon*, placed there by his grandsons.

On the corner of Craven and Broad Streets stands the oldest church in Beaufort, called Purvis Chapel. This church was built in 1820 and originally stood on the corner of Ann and Craven Streets, but when the new Methodist church was built, the Purvis Chapel was moved to its present site and given to the colored people. It is used today, and the original bell cast in Glasgow, Scotland, in 1790 rings out every Sunday.

Map of downtown Beaufort, 1830. *Courtesy of the Beaufort Historical Association.*

We move down Craven Street and see a small two-story brick building, built in 1832, on the square. Designated as county property as a jail, it was in use until 1954. There is a story told about a commissioners' meeting, when one commissioner made a motion that they build a new jail. The mayor said, "What in the world do we want with a new jail?" The commissioner answered, "So we can get a better clientele." That was in 1854, and in 1954, the town fathers got around to carrying out the motion. So after one hundred years, the new brick building on our left is a result of the speed with which Beaufort people proceed.

We turn the corner of Cedar Street and head west. We stop here for a few minutes to hear about the three people who were hanged in Beaufort for capital crimes. We notice the stocks outside the old jail, and if we get out of the bus, we can see an eyebolt screwed over the sill of the front door. One of the criminals was hanged there. We also see a huge oak tree on the square. This tree is called the "Talking and Hanging Tree." Here another one of the criminals, a man named Drummert, was hanged. He was convicted of rape, but many Beaufort citizens thought he was innocent. Such was the feeling about this that a jury had to be sent from Jones County for the trial. Drummert was convicted as charged, and was hanged on the oak tree on the square. For years, the townsfolk said you could go and tap on the old tree and say, "What did they hang Drummert for?" and the tree would say, "Nothing." The other hanging took place on a scaffold near the oldest courthouse on Turner Street.

On Cedar Street, we pass by historical markers. The first says that the Revolutionary forces had saltworks in the eastern part of Beaufort. Salt was such a valuable product that, as early as 1722, the people were permitted to pay their taxes with salt. The solar method of extracting salt from the ocean water was used.

The second marker says that the Spanish landed and captured Beaufort in 1747. They were repelled by the local citizens and farmers from out in the county. Beaufort was under the Spanish flag for only a few days.

The third marker says that on Shackleford Banks a whale fishery was established in 1724, started by Samuel Chadwick. This was the first whale fishery south of the New England coast.

We now turn on Turner Street, the street that Robert Turner named for himself back in 1719, when he bought his land from Nathaniel Green. This street was supposed to be the hub of activity for a dream city he had in mind. We see a red brick building on our left as we head south toward the water. This is the Odd Fellows Lodge and was built in 1837.

It was constructed at night by torchlight as a labor of love by the Masons, who built Fort Macon by day. Every other row of bricks stands on end and goes though the wall so that the plaster on the inside makes a rigid form of construction.

On the left-hand corner of Turner and Ann Streets, we see a house built of heart pine, one and a half stories high. This house originally stood in the center of Ann Street, here at this corner, and was the third courthouse in Beaufort. It was built around 1796 and was called the Hall of Justice. This house was also used as a customs house. Beaufort became a port of entry in 1723, and the stagecoaches used this as their stopping place. We are reminded that in the early days of Beaufort this street had an auction block where captured Indians, as well as Negroes, were sold. The best of the slaves were sold for fifty dollars, but the Indians were most unsatisfactory as slaves. They refused to work in homes or outside, regardless of punishment.

Times moved slowly, but the harbor was filled with sailing vessels from the North, the Bahamas and even across the Atlantic. Sometimes as many as a hundred sailing vessels could be seen in the harbor. It was a little different as far as land travel was concerned. Roads were terrible, when there were roads. Distances were great and means of travel was difficult. A man from Straits was elected to the legislature. He started out on mule back, since this was his only means of travel, but when he arrived at the capital, he found the legislature had already sat and adjourned. Such was Beaufort's isolation.

Two very old houses on Turner Street, we are told, have been bought by the historical association for restoration. The one of the left, called the Josiah Bell House, was built in 1832. This at one time was the home of the postmaster who figured so tragically in the story of Nancy Manney.

The other house on the right on Turner Street was built in 1767. This house has been completely restored and furnished with antiques of the period. Most of the valuable furnishings were donated, and the garden was planted by the Garden Club of Beaufort. The stones used as foundation for this house were previously used as ballast for sailing ships. Many Beaufort homes used ballast stones in this way.

Now we turn to the north on Orange Street. This street was named for Prince William of Orange, who later became king of England. The house on the corner on the left was built in 1770. One of the stipulations when building a house was that it had to be fifteen by twenty feet with an outside chimney. This house is much larger now, and the places where additions were made can easily be seen. This house is three stories with a basement that also has a fireplace and is quite livable. The house was at one time owned by the first Jewish man sent to the North Carolina Legislature. In 1840, the house was sold to Marcus Thomas and was in the Thomas family until 1954, when the last Thomas owner died. He willed the house to John Jones, who lives there now.

During the Civil War, this house was taken over by the Federal forces and some of the Federal soldiers were billeted there. After the fall of Fort Macon, Confederate prisoners were brought over to Beaufort and were imprisoned in the basement of this house. There were iron bars on all the basement windows, but the windows were level with the street. There were a number of young ladies living next door who formed a group to aid the soldiers and prisoners. One of these ladies was Fannie Styron from Davis Shore, who took an interest in one prisoner. This friendship developed into love and marriage after the war. This particular soldier happened to be Raymond Luther Paul, our guide's grandfather.

Just a little down Orange Street on the left side of the street is another house built before the Civil War. This house was the home of Charity Fuller. Fuller was a name well known in the early days of Beaufort history. Charity Fuller had a son who was stationed at Fort Macon, and she and some of her friends stood on the upper piazza, tensely and prayerfully watching through binoculars the bombarding of Fort Macon. Emmeline Piggot, the famous Confederate spy, was also visiting here at this time. She was most attractive and managed to use her charm to secure military secrets from the Federal soldiers.

We now turn west on Ann Street. The house over on the northeast corner of Ann and Orange Streets was built before the Civil War and is known as the Lee Craft House. This house was also taken over by the Federal forces and was occupied by the provost marshal. The axe marks can still be seen on the heart pine floors in the kitchen and dining room, where it was said that the solders cut up the apple and cherry trees in the yard to use for firewood.

A little farther down toward the east on Ann Street is a house known as Ma Taylor's. She died recently at the age of 104. Her home was always open to welcome her friends during her long life.

Across the street from her home is a house that was used as a hospital during the war. It was originally built for a hotel, and guests of great prominence from all over the territory stayed here.

Proceeding toward the west on Ann Street we see the St. Paul's Episcopal Church, which was built in 1857. It is noteworthy that all three of the oldest churches in Beaufort—the Baptist (built in 1853; it has since been torn down and replaced with a new building), the Methodist (in 1854) and the Episcopal (in 1857)—were built just prior to the Civil War, which seems to indicate that there must have been a revival of religion as well as an economic boom.

The house on the north corner of Ann and Moore Streets was built and lived in by James W. Davis, an architect and engineer. He built over twenty-two houses in Beaufort prior to

Leecraft House. *Courtesy of the Beaufort Historical Association.*

the Civil War. He also lived in another house down on Moore Street and had his cabinet shop in the basement. Many of the old houses in Beaufort have mantels and cabinets built by James Davis before 1834.

In this next block on Ann Street, west to the water from Moore Street, many of the houses were built in 1771, before the Revolutionary War. Peter Piver built the small house on the north corner. This little house has a slanting roof like many others in Beaufort, but is only one story. Some of the

James W. Davis House. *Courtesy of the Beaufort Historical Association.*

floorboards are sixteen inches wide, one and a quarter inches thick and are made of native heart pine. Peter Piver, his son and his grandson all fought in the Revolutionary War.

Near this house is one called the Robert Chadwick House, also built by James W. Davis. A little girl died here of yellow fever during the Civil War and it took the Federal authorities, who were in command of Beaufort then, three days to get permission to bury the child.

Another house of interest on this block is the William Jackson Potter house. Because public schools were not in existence yet, this house was used for a private school for young ladies.

On the south side of Ann on this same block is the Buckman House, built in the early 1800s. This house was built in the style of houses in Louisiana.

Another James W. Davis design. *Courtesy of the Beaufort Historical Association.*

Next to this house is a house that is also called the Buckman House, but many additions have been added and the original part of the house is so old that the date has been lost in antiquity. This was Ma Taylor's girlhood home.

The Methodists built the next house as a parsonage in 1820, the same year the Purvis Chapel was built.

We turn now on Moore Street, heading south. The second house on the left is the old St. Paul's Rectory, now a privately owned home. Paul Green, our own North Carolina playwright, courted Elizabeth, the eldest daughter of Dr. and Mrs. Lay. Dr. Lay was the rector of St. Paul's Church at that time. The wedding reception was held in the beautiful garden that Mrs. Lay had nurtured with loving care.

As we approach the last house on our left facing the water, we notice that the doors and windows are not centered. This house was built by Perry Nelson, a ship's carpenter. It has been said that his house is very much like the house Tara,

Leslie Davis House. *Courtesy of the Beaufort Historical Association.*

used in the movie *Gone with the Wind*. The overhanging roof covering the porch is typical of most of the old houses in Beaufort.

We turn the corner here to the right, to a long, rambling house that is really three houses joined together. This is known as the old Leslie Davis House. It was used as a hotel for many years in the 1800s, and until a few years ago, people from all over North Carolina came to spend their summers here, resting in the rocking chairs that lined the porch, watching the children playing in the water and enjoying the delicious food that was served. From the docks in front they went by sharpie to the ocean beaches and Shackleford Banks.

At the end of this street is the Captain Duncan House. This house, too, was built by James Davis. There are two sections to the house; one was used as living quarters and the other as a store, since most of the people in Beaufort made their living from the water by shipping. Some sailed the seas carrying naval stores from this section, and bringing back sugar, cloth and other necessary supplies. This section of the world carried on a thriving business with the Bahamas. Thomas Duncan noticed the high price of the boxes that brought in the sugar and decided that since native pine was so plentiful here, he would make his own boxes to bring back the sugar. The boxes were sent down to the Bahamas, where the sugar was loaded in the boxes and brought back to Beaufort. The inspectors came, sampled the sugar and discovered that the turpentine had seeped out of the raw pine boxes, ruining the sugar. The whole cargo had to be destroyed. Our guide said it was a good thing his grandmother wasn't living then, because she would have bottled all the sugar and sold it for medicine, since she always treated all the children with sugar and turpentine for sore throats.

We are still on Front Street, and the location of an interesting house is pointed out to us on the site of the present Jule Duncan House. James W. Cooke was a very enterprising young man. He joined the navy and was commissioned as a midshipman. When the Civil War broke out, he resigned his commissions, joined the Confederate navy and became captain of the famous ram ironclad the *Albemarle*, which fought in the famous Battle of Plymouth.

Over on the left are other houses facing the water. Most of the hoses in Beaufort are surrounded by white picket fences to keep the geese, cattle and sheep from wandering, and to protect the flowers and gardens. In the Morse House there is a solid marble mantel imported in the early days from Europe. There is a similar one in Ma Taylor's House.

Duncan House. *Courtesy of the Beaufort Historical Association.*

Across from the Thomas House, which we heard about in the beginning of our tour, is another old house, the Murray Thomas House. It has an odd number of columns and off-centered doors and steps. The basement is built above ground, but was to offer protection from the rising tides. Basements were not usually dug down in the ground, and the house was a three-story affair, with the basement on the first floor.

The next house is known as the Cedars. It gets its name from the windswept trees in the front yard, which you can readily see, leaned back from the prevailing sou'westers for these hundreds of years. Of course they are mostly stumps now; only one of them is left, but there was a time when numbers of living cedars sloped back with the wind and made a fine place for a boy to walk up the trunks. This house was built by one of the original French Huguenots who helped to settle Beaufort. His name was Parne. His great-great-grandson was John Hones, who owned the famous Octagon House in Swansboro. The builder said he wanted a house so that the sou'westers wouldn't whistle around the corners.

The next house on the left is one of the many haunted houses in Beaufort. They all have a story behind them. A man lived there by the name of Captain John Sabiston, and his wife was called Miss Mattie. Captain John was a seafaring man, like most of the men in Beaufort. They would go out on cruises that would sometimes last for six months. It was nothing unusual for ships to be gone for a long time. Whenever a ship came into port, everyone would go to see if the returning seamen had heard anything from their loved ones at sea. They didn't have docks in these days; they anchored the big boats out in the channel and then came ashore in little skiffs. They just tied the skiffs to posts and walked up to the landing. One night Miss Mattie heard a commotion out in front of the house and thought it was Captain John coming up the landing with a lantern in his hand. She thought he must have gone around to the back, so she went around to the back door and called, "John, John," but no one answered. Finally she thought it must have been a bad dream. She went back upstairs and tried to go to sleep, but needless to say she didn't sleep much that night.

About two or three weeks later another ship came in, captained by Captain Jim Ireland. As was the custom, everybody went down to the water to see the ship come in and inquire as to whether the seamen had heard anything from their friends. When Captain Ireland saw Miss Mattie coming he knew what he had to do. She came right up to him and asked, "Captain Jim, have you seen anything of my husband? Do you know where his ship is?" He said, "Miss Mattie, I am sorry to tell you, but two weeks ago tonight your husband's ship was lost with all twenty-two men aboard."

The night of his wreck was the very same night she had had the dream. This was told as a true story, but it is also told that oftentimes on a real calm night you can year Captain John walking up the steps, coming toward the house with a lantern in his hand. This is just one of the many "haunted" houses in Beaufort.

We pass through our busiest business block in Beaufort and now we see on the left the Lena Duncan House. It was built by Langdon back in 1854. There is something interesting about this house. Notice it is three stories too, but the three stories had a purpose. It was used as a schoolhouse. It was first known as Beaufort Female Academy, the first paying school established in Beaufort for women. This house has been in the Duncan family since it was first built.

The house on the next left, one story with two dormer windows, is known as the Mattie Duncan House and was supposed to have been built by John White, a direct descendant of John White of famous Roanoke Island history and the lost colony.

Turning the corner on Pollock Street, we notice an iron marker. This is the dividing line between "Old Town" and "New Town." When Robert Turner had his land surveyed and streets laid off for the town of Beaufort, this is as far east as he had surveyed. There are many homes past this marker toward the east that are as old as any in Old Town, many built before the Revolution, but the incorporated limits back in 1722 only extended this far. Pollock Street was named for the earl of Craven's right-hand man. Pollock later became governor of North Carolina.

On the northwest corner of Pollock and Ann Streets is the Mace House. This house was built in 1840. It has the original pine doors and floors. Some of the fine furniture now in use has been used by four or five generations, and some of it was bought for this house. Notice the overhanging roof used in building so many of the houses in Beaufort.

As we turn on Queen Street, the second house on our left is known as the Allen Davis House. This house was occupied by General Ambrose E. Burnside during the Civil War. Burnside wore his hair long on each side of his face, and was responsible for creating the style now known as "sideburns." He was commanding general of all the Federal forces in eastern North Carolina at the time when Fort Macon fell. It was said that General Burnside was a pretty hardhearted man, but this story told about him proves this untrue.

When Fort Macon fell, two of the men who died in the fort were from Beaufort. One was named Jehochihum Davis, and he is buried in Beaufort's old cemetery. When the prisoners were brought over to Beaufort after Fort Macon had fallen, this one man was in his casket. People had gone down to the water's edge to see the prisoners, and Davis's mother and father were there too. Captain Burnside was there, in his official capacity. As the casket was taken off the boat, General Burnside went over and offered his condolences to Davis's mother and father. It was said that tears could be seen rolling down his sunburned cheeks.

As we turn back on Front Street, we are told to watch for the wild marsh ponies across on the shoal. They are descendants of Arabian studs, the finest horses in the world, that were shipwrecked on the Outer Banks over two hundred years ago. These horses kept getting smaller and smaller until they got down to the size of a Shetland pony, but in the last thirty years or so they have been taken care of and their size has increased. In the early 1970s, the State of North Carolina passed a law compelling them to be taken off the Outer Banks because it was thought that they were destroying the grass and causing erosion. Some of the

Mace House. *Courtesy of the Beaufort Historical Association.*

horses have been taken to Cedar Island, and they have pony pennings two or three times a year, usually on July 4. They were put on Carrot Island about five or six years ago. The strange thing about these horses is that they will never swim to the mainland, but they swim over the deep creeks against the strongest tides, from one island to another.

The old sharpie you see beached at the end of Pollock Street on the water side is a typical sailing boat that has been used for 250 years. Now it is being used as a museum. The boat itself is a relic because there is none other like it today. Inside the boat are relics of bygone days and old fishermen's tools, especially tools of the whaling industry that were used on Shackleford Banks.

Farther down on Front Street, toward the east, there are three houses that look very much the same. These are the Gladys Chadwick, A.W. Daniels and the Hill homes.

These houses all were built under stipulations and are pre–Revolutionary War houses.

On Marsh Street we see two very old houses, one owned by Mrs. Cora Russell. This house has an interesting cupola, and the interior work was done by a ship's carpenter, and the trim in the living room came from a ship. The stairs are so constructed that they have no visible means of support. The house sold in 1779 for a cow and a calf. Many prominent people have lived in this house, including a well-known writer, a state representative and a U.S. senator. The other house, built in 1772 and called the Rumley House, was the home of Beaufort's beloved Circuit Rider minister, Reverend James Rumley.

On the east corner of Live Oak and Front Streets is the Gibbs House. This is the first house in Beaufort built of any lumber other than pine. This house was built of cypress and juniper cut in Hyde County, and brought here by a relative named Ramsey. He said he was going to build his house so it would last a hundred years or longer. He put his house together with copper nails. All the other old houses in Beaufort were put together with wooden pegs or iron nails, hammered out one by one. This house really did last, needing very little repair during its existence. The front steps have recently been replaced after all these years, and the new ones are already beginning to rot after only a few years.

Really, the oldest house in Beaufort is the Hammock House. We won't tell the history of this house here, as we have a full story about it elsewhere in this publication. This is surely one house that is haunted. But it's time to return our guests to their destination.

Now I, Grayden Paul, your tour guide of this beautiful town, would like to tell you in poetry how I was inspired, by the lives of those who have lived, loved and died in Beaufort, to write these lines, which I call "The Fisherman."

POEMS BY THE PAULS

THE FISHERMAN

Many a lonely heart has lingered
On these sandy windswept shores,
Waiting, hoping, crying, praying,
While their loved ones, bending oars,
Struggled fiercely in the tempest,
Carrying out a seaman's chores.
But at last a mast is sighted
In the early morning haze,
And those weary hearts grow lighter
With the thoughts of brighter days.
When the seamen, again united
With their families hand in hand,
Kneel and thank the Master Pilot;
Lord of Heaven, Sea and Sand.

A View from My Window on Taylor's Creek

I have seen the Marsh-hen swimming
With her young on Taylor's Creek.
I have seen a Curlew running,
Catch a minnow in its beak.

I have seen the Great Blue Heron
With its neck and legs extreme
Standing like a painted statue
On the border of the stream.

Then there comes a sudden motion
As the Blue Crab saunters by,
When the Heron spears his breakfast,
And hold him jauntily to the sky.

There's no other bird so cunning
As this mammoth of them all,
Though his little cousin, Egret,
Could Surely answer second call.

O, how well do I remember,
And 'twas not so long ago.
Taylor's Creek was filled with porpoise
Gaily swimming to and fro.

But now the water seems polluted,
And this wise old dolphin knows
How to miss the lurking danger,
So off to cleaner water goes.

Yes, I've seen the might Eagle
Spread his wings against the sky;

But it, too, is disappearing
And I often wonder why.

My little friend the Sea Chick
Has returned to spend the day,
Searching for his favorite seafood
In the cracks along the quay.

You should see his sly maneuvering
As he flits along the pier,
Scaring out his favorite morsels,
Then he stabs them with his spear.

On a calm and peaceful morning
When the wind is from the land,
Taylor's Creek is one big mirror
Reflecting trees and marsh and sand.

Then again, the wind is blowing
With all its fury and its might,
And you feel so small and helpless
As you shudder through the night.

But soon you see that dawn is breaking;
And with every rising sun
Comes the miracle of Nature
Whose work of art is never done.

All the things that I have mentioned
Are the handy works of God;
But man, too, must add his touches,
Ere he sleeps beneath the sod.

So I look beyond my window,
Out to Beaufort Inlet Bar,
Where many ocean ships are sailing
With their cargoes from afar.

Then I hear the roar of motors
As a jet goes streaking by,
But all I see is trails of vapor
Painting pictures in the sky.

When I finally get to Heaven
And walk along those golden streets
I hope to see cedar and yaupon
Such as grows on Taylor's Creek.

∽

A PRAYER FOR OUR COUNTRY
written in 1954 in connection with the International Sunday School
lessons; it is very appropriate now, as we approach our bicentennial
celebration

O Lord God, of all creation
Whose mighty arms hold sway.
Grant us strength to meet the challenge
Of his fast and furious day.

Lest Thy patience be exhausted
And Thy Holy wrath descend
On this blind and sinful nation,
Bringing us a woeful end.

Lord, we know the fact of history,
That all nations gone before
Who have failed to heed Thy teachings,
Have been lost forevermore.

Yet, we think we hold the secret
Of a nation ruled by man,
That can make its own Salvation,
O, how little we understand!

Our founding fathers had a vision
Of a nation built to stand
Under strain and stress of hardships,
Depending on Thy guiding hand.

But in modern times we've drifted,
Lured by money, fame and power,
Groping on in sin and darkness,
While Thy blessings, 'round us shower

Spare us, Lord, from self-destruction
Such as ancient Israel saw,
Sinking farther into darkness
By defiance of Thy Law.

Stop us now, for time is fleeting,
Help us Lord to understand,
That Thy son who died on Calvary
Is the answer, not mere man.

Yea, Lord God, we pray for mercy,
A stay of judgment in our time,
That we may learn Thine oft-taught lesson
And bend our wills like unto Thine.

A SUBSTITUTE FOR SLEEPING PILLS

As the whippoorwill coos in the evening breeze,
And the wind murmurs softly through the dunes and trees,
Comes a soothing respite from the heat of the day,
And a nearness to God, as you kneel to pray.

Then your mind wanders back through the turmoil and strife,
Which is man's common lot in this earthly bound life,
And you're thankful to God for His Infinite Love,
And a plan for His children is a better home above.
Away with your bottle of Sleeping Pills
And your dreadful fear of imaginary ills,
Then comes the comforting mantle of sleep,
And your soul is at rest as you lay at His feet.

Old Folk Songs

The Battle Ship *Maine*

(first stanza)
Many homes were filled with sorrow and with sadness.
Many hearts were torn with anguish and with pain;
And our Country lay engulfed with grief and sorry
For our heroes on the Battleship, the Maine.
Oh, the moon shone out that night across the water
And the heroes of our Maine *in silence lay,*
For two hundred noble hearted sailors perished
On the shores of Havana far away.

(second stanza)
Some were thinking of their mothers, wives and sweethearts.
Some were thinking of their loved ones left at home;
And perhaps some lad had left his old folks grieving
And was writing them from far across the foam.
When suddenly!—there came a loud explosion,
Like a stony wreck she sank down in the bay;
And two hundred noble hearted sailors perished
On the shores of Havana far away.

❧

PLEASE, MR. CONDUCTOR

Please, Mr. Conductor,
Don't put me off of the train;
For the best friend I have in this world, sir,
Lies waiting for me in pain.
Expected to die any moment,
She may not last through the day.
I want to kiss Mama good-bye, Sir,
Before God takes her away.

❧

THE WEEPING WILLOW TREE

(first stanza)
My heart is sad and I am lonely
For the one I love is gone.
She's gone, she's gone to see another;
She no longer cares for me.

(chorus)
Go bury me beneath the Tree,
Beneath the weeping will tree;
And when she knows that I am sleeping,
Then perhaps she'll think of me.

(second stanza)
Tomorrow is my wedding day
I pray to the Lord; where is my love.
If I never see her on earth again
I hope to meet her in Heaven above.

(third stanza)
She told me that she did not love me
Still I did not believe it true,
Until an angel whispered softly,
"She no longer cares for you."

౼

THE DYING FIFER

In the battle hot and raging
While the shots and shells did fly
All around the rigging hurling
Lo, I heard a piercing cry.
There beside me lay our Fifer*
From his bosom spouted blood.
There he lay pierced by a bullet
Dying in the crimson flood.
He said, "Shipmate, tell my father,
Tell him I died like a man;
Died in battle for my Country
While blood around in torrents ran.
Tell my mother, gently tell her;
Lest this news should break her heart;

That her son will one day meet her
Where we never more shall part.
Tell my brothers, yes my brothers
On Santiago's sunny shore,*
That our battles are victorious
And shall be forevermore.
Tell my sister, I remember
Every kind important word,

And my heart has been kept tender
By the thoughts her memory stirred."
The he paused and ceased from speaking,
Gently yielding up his breath.
A heavenly smile lit up his features
As he closed his eyes in death.

*Fife—small musical instrument of the flute kind, having but one key and a compass of two octaves; major, a noncommissioned officer who superintends the fifers of a battalion
*Santiago—seaport city in Cuba; site of battles in 1898

⁂

WHERE DID YOU GET THAT HAT?

(first stanza)
At twenty-one, I thought I would
To my sweetheart get married.
The people in the neighborhood
Had said, "Too long we'd tarried."
So quickly to the Church we went
Expecting to get wed.
No sooner had we got there, than
The parson to me said—

(chorus)
"Where did you get that hat?
Where did you get that tie?
Oh, isn't it a pretty one;
It's just the proper style.
Oh, I would like to have one

Just the same as that."
Were e'er I go, they shout, "Hello,
Where did you get that hat?"

(second stanza)
If we should go to the opera house
In the opera season
Someone there'd be sure to laugh
Without the slightest reason.
If we should go to the dancing hall
To have a little spree
Someone in the parlor there
Would be sure to shout at me—

(chorus)

Visit us at
www.historypress.net

www.ingramcontent.com/pod-product-compliance
Lightning Source LLC
Chambersburg PA
CBHW060751100426
42813CB00004B/775